Title: The Curious Mind: A Journey into AI

Table of Contents:

Chapter 1: The Spark of Curiosity
Song: "What a Wonderful World" by Louis Armstrong

Curiosity begins with asking questions. This chapter explores how to ignite curiosity in the realm of AI. Learn to view AI as a puzzle waiting to be solved rather than a daunting field. Understand that every innovation starts with a question.

Tips and Techniques:

1. **Ask Questions:** Start by asking basic questions about AI and its applications.
2. **Read Widely:** Explore various resources, from articles to books, to understand the broad landscape of AI.

Chapter 2: Embrace the Basics
Song: "Here Comes the Sun" by The Beatles

Dive into the foundational concepts of AI, including machine learning, neural networks, and data science. Understanding these basics is crucial for building a solid foundation.

Tips and Techniques:

1. **Interactive Learning:** Use online platforms that offer interactive AI courses.
2. **Hands-On Projects:** Start small projects to apply what you've learned.

Chapter 3: The Joy of Problem-Solving
Song: "Eye of the Tiger" by Survivor

AI is all about solving problems. Learn how to approach problems methodically and embrace challenges as opportunities for growth. This chapter highlights the joy and satisfaction that comes with solving complex problems.

Tips and Techniques:

1. **Break Down Problems:** Tackle complex problems by breaking them into smaller, manageable parts.
2. **Seek Feedback:** Share your solutions with others to get different perspectives.

Chapter 4: The Power of Patterns
Song: "Shape of You" by Ed Sheeran

AI often involves recognizing patterns in data. Explore how identifying and understanding patterns can lead to breakthroughs in AI. This chapter explains the significance of pattern recognition and its role in machine learning.

Tips and Techniques:

1. **Visualize Data:** Use tools to visualize data and recognize patterns.
2. **Experiment with Algorithms:** Try different algorithms to see how they handle patterns in data.

Chapter 5: The Importance of Data
Song: "Counting Stars" by OneRepublic

Data is the backbone of AI. Learn about the types of data used in AI and how to collect, clean, and analyze data effectively. This chapter emphasizes the role of data in training AI models.

Tips and Techniques:

1. **Understand Data Sources:** Learn where to find and how to use different types of data.
2. **Data Cleaning:** Develop skills in cleaning and preprocessing data to improve model performance.

Chapter 6: Experimentation and Innovation
Song: "Rocket Man" by Elton John

Innovation in AI comes from experimentation. This chapter encourages experimenting with different models and approaches to discover what works best for your projects.

Tips and Techniques:

1. **Try Different Models:** Experiment with various AI models to find the best fit for your problem.
2. **Stay Updated:** Keep up with the latest research and trends in AI.

Chapter 7: Collaboration and Community
Song: "Lean on Me" by Bill Withers

AI is a collaborative field. Join communities, participate in forums, and collaborate with others to share knowledge and gain new insights.

Tips and Techniques:

1. **Join Online Communities:** Engage with AI communities and forums to learn from others.
2. **Attend Meetups and Conferences:** Participate in events to network and exchange ideas.

Chapter 8: The Role of Ethics
Song: "Imagine" by John Lennon

Ethics in AI is crucial. Understand the ethical implications of AI and how to develop responsible AI systems. This chapter highlights the importance of ethical considerations in AI development.

Tips and Techniques:

1. **Study AI Ethics:** Learn about ethical guidelines and frameworks for AI.
2. **Consider Impacts:** Think about how AI solutions affect individuals and society.

Chapter 9: The Future of AI
Song: "Don't Stop Believin'" by Journey

AI is a rapidly evolving field. Stay curious about emerging technologies and future trends. This chapter explores the potential future directions of AI and how to stay engaged with its advancements.

Tips and Techniques:

1. **Follow Innovations:** Keep an eye on cutting-edge technologies and their implications.
2. **Be Adaptive:** Be ready to adapt and learn as AI continues to evolve.

Chapter 10: Cultivating a Lifelong Curiosity
Song: "Forever Young" by Bob Dylan

Curiosity is a lifelong journey. Develop a mindset that fosters continuous learning and growth in AI. This chapter provides strategies for maintaining curiosity and enthusiasm over the long term.

Tips and Techniques:

1. **Set Learning Goals:** Continuously set new goals to keep your learning journey exciting.
2. **Reflect and Iterate:** Regularly reflect on your progress and iterate on your learning strategies.

Formula for Developing a Curious Mindset:

1. **Start Small:** Begin with basic concepts and gradually move to more advanced topics.

2. **Stay Engaged:** Regularly update yourself with the latest trends and innovations.
3. **Embrace Challenges:** View obstacles as opportunities for learning and growth.
4. **Seek Inspiration:** Find mentors, join communities, and be inspired by others' work.
5. **Reflect Often:** Regularly assess your progress and adjust your learning strategies.

Mindset Development Tips:

- **Passion Over Perfection:** Focus on your passion for learning rather than striving for perfection.
- **Curiosity as a Habit:** Make curiosity a daily habit by dedicating time to explore new ideas and technologies.
- **Resilience:** Develop resilience to overcome setbacks and continue your learning journey.

This novel provides a roadmap for nurturing curiosity and advancing from a layman's perspective to a more advanced understanding of AI. By following the tips, techniques, and mindset development strategies, readers can embark on a fulfilling journey into the world of artificial intelligence

Chapter 1: The Spark of Curiosity

Song: "What a Wonderful World" by Louis Armstrong

Curiosity is the cornerstone of discovery and innovation. It's the driving force that pushes us to explore, learn, and grow. In the realm of Artificial Intelligence (AI), curiosity is not just about understanding complex algorithms or high-tech applications but about recognizing the potential of this field and asking the right questions. This chapter is about igniting that spark of curiosity and transforming it into a passion for learning.

Understanding Curiosity in AI

Curiosity in AI begins with recognizing that AI is not a monolithic field but a vast and evolving domain. It encompasses various aspects like machine learning, neural networks, natural language processing, robotics, and more. To truly understand AI, one must first appreciate that it's a collection of interconnected puzzles, each waiting to be explored.

1. Embracing the Puzzle Metaphor

Imagine AI as a gigantic, intricate puzzle. Each piece represents a different technology or concept within AI. Some pieces are easy to fit, while others require a bit of experimentation and thought. Your goal is to piece together these parts to see the bigger picture. Just like solving a puzzle, the process requires patience, exploration, and, most importantly, a curious mindset.

2. The Power of Questions

Every great advancement begins with a question. For instance, the question, "How can we teach machines to recognize speech?" led to the development of voice assistants. Similarly, asking, "What if we could predict stock market trends using AI?" has driven advancements in financial technologies.

3. Viewing AI as an Opportunity

Instead of seeing AI as a daunting field filled with complex mathematics and programming, approach it as a realm full of opportunities. AI can transform industries, solve real-world problems, and create innovative solutions. Your curiosity can lead you to discover new ways to apply AI to various challenges.

Tips and Techniques to Ignite Curiosity

1. Ask Questions

Start with basic questions to build a foundational understanding. Here are some examples:

- **What is AI?** Understand the basic concept and its different subfields.
- **How does machine learning work?** Learn about the process of training algorithms to make predictions.
- **What are neural networks?** Explore how these models attempt to mimic human brain functions.
- **What are the applications of AI?** Identify where AI is being used today, from recommendation systems to autonomous vehicles.

Asking questions not only clarifies your understanding but also guides your learning journey.

2. Read Widely

Expand your knowledge by exploring various resources. Each type of material offers different insights into AI:

- **Books:** Start with foundational texts like "Artificial Intelligence: A Modern Approach" by Stuart Russell and Peter Norvig. These books provide comprehensive overviews and are essential for building a strong base.

- **Articles and Blogs:** Read articles on platforms like Medium, Towards Data Science, and Arxiv to keep up with the latest trends and research in AI.

- **Research Papers:** For a deeper understanding, delve into research papers available on Google Scholar or academic journals. Papers provide insights into cutting-edge developments and methodologies.

- **Online Courses:** Enroll in online courses from platforms like Coursera, edX, or Udacity. Many of these courses offer interactive learning experiences and practical applications.

3. Engage with AI Communities

Join online forums, social media groups, or local meetups dedicated to AI. Engaging with others interested in AI can provide new perspectives, answer questions, and keep you motivated.

- **Reddit:** Subreddits like r/MachineLearning and r/ArtificialIntelligence are great for discussions and learning about the latest trends.

- **LinkedIn:** Follow AI professionals and companies to stay updated with industry news and developments.

- **Meetups:** Attend local AI meetups or webinars to network with like-minded individuals and learn from experts.

4. Start Small Projects

Apply what you've learned through small projects. For instance:

- **Build a Simple Chatbot:** Use platforms like Dialogflow or IBM Watson to create a basic chatbot.

- **Analyze Data:** Work with datasets from Kaggle or UCI Machine Learning Repository to practice data analysis and model building.

- **Implement Algorithms:** Try implementing basic machine learning algorithms from scratch to understand their workings.

Small projects can provide practical experience and help solidify your understanding.

Building a Curiosity-Driven Mindset

To maintain and grow your curiosity, consider these strategies:

- **Set Learning Goals:** Establish clear, achievable goals for what you want to learn about AI. This could be mastering a particular algorithm or understanding a new application.

- **Stay Persistent:** Curiosity is fueled by persistence. Don't be discouraged by challenges; view them as opportunities to learn and grow.

- **Reflect and Iterate:** Regularly reflect on what you've learned and how you can build on it. Adjust your learning approach based on what works best for you.

Summary

In this chapter, you've begun the journey of transforming curiosity into a passion for learning AI. By asking questions, exploring diverse resources, and engaging with the AI community, you lay the groundwork for a deeper understanding of this exciting field. Embrace the challenge and enjoy the process of discovering how AI can transform the world.

As you progress through this book, remember that curiosity is your most valuable asset. It's the key to unlocking new ideas and innovations, and it will guide you through your journey in the fascinating world of AI.

Next up in Chapter 2: **"Embrace the Basics"** – where you'll dive into foundational AI concepts and start building your knowledge base. Stay curious, and keep exploring!

Chapter 2: Embrace the Basics

Song: "Here Comes the Sun" by The Beatles

As we venture deeper into the world of Artificial Intelligence (AI), it's essential to lay a solid foundation. This chapter is about embracing and understanding the core concepts of AI, which will serve as the bedrock for more advanced topics. By grasping these basics, you'll be better equipped to tackle more complex ideas and applications.

Understanding the Core Concepts of AI

1. **Machine Learning (ML)**

Machine Learning is a subset of AI focused on teaching machines to learn from data and make decisions without being explicitly programmed. ML algorithms use statistical techniques to identify patterns and make predictions. There are several types of machine learning:

- **Supervised Learning:** The model is trained on labeled data, meaning the outcomes are known. For example, predicting house prices based on historical data.

- **Unsupervised Learning:** The model is trained on unlabeled data and must find hidden patterns or intrinsic structures. For instance, clustering customers into segments based on their buying behavior.

- **Reinforcement Learning:** The model learns through interactions with an environment, receiving rewards or penalties. It's used in applications like game playing and autonomous vehicles.

2. **Neural Networks**

Neural Networks are a key component of deep learning, which is a subset of machine learning. They are inspired by the human brain and consist of layers of interconnected nodes (neurons). Neural networks are used for complex tasks such as image recognition, natural language processing, and speech recognition.

- **Feedforward Neural Networks:** Information moves in one direction, from input to output.
- **Convolutional Neural Networks (CNNs):** Specialized for processing structured grid data like images. They are excellent for image and video recognition tasks.
- **Recurrent Neural Networks (RNNs):** Designed for sequential data and time series. They are useful for tasks such as language modeling and speech recognition.

3. **Data Science**

Data Science is the process of extracting insights from large amounts of data. It involves various steps, including data collection, data cleaning, exploratory data analysis, and modeling.

- **Data Collection:** Gathering raw data from different sources.
- **Data Cleaning:** Removing or correcting inaccuracies and inconsistencies in the data.
- **Exploratory Data Analysis (EDA):** Analyzing data sets to summarize their main characteristics, often with visual methods.
- **Modeling:** Applying statistical and machine learning models to data to make predictions or understand patterns.

Tips and Techniques to Embrace the Basics

1. Interactive Learning

Interactive learning platforms offer a hands-on approach to grasping AI concepts. Here's how you can leverage these resources:

- **Online Courses:** Platforms like Coursera, edX, and Udacity offer interactive courses on AI and machine learning. These courses often include video lectures, quizzes, and coding assignments.
- **Interactive Notebooks:** Use Jupyter Notebooks or Google Colab to experiment with code snippets and visualize results. These tools provide an interactive environment where you can write and execute code in real-time.
- **Coding Challenges:** Websites like Kaggle and HackerRank offer coding challenges and competitions that help you apply AI concepts in practical scenarios.

2. Hands-On Projects

Applying what you've learned through small projects is crucial for solidifying your understanding. Here's how you can get started:

- **Build a Simple ML Model:** Start by building a basic model using a dataset from Kaggle or UCI Machine Learning Repository. For example, create a model to predict house prices or classify flowers based on their attributes.
- **Develop a Neural Network:** Use frameworks like TensorFlow or PyTorch to create a simple neural network for tasks such as digit recognition (MNIST dataset) or sentiment analysis.
- **Analyze Real-World Data:** Download datasets from sources like government databases or public APIs and perform exploratory data analysis. Try to uncover insights or trends from the data.

3. Explore and Experiment

- **Experiment with Different Algorithms:** Don't stick to just one algorithm. Try different machine learning and neural network algorithms to understand their strengths and weaknesses.
- **Visualize Data:** Use visualization tools like Matplotlib or Seaborn to create charts and graphs. Visualizing data helps in understanding patterns and relationships.

4. Learn from Mistakes

- **Debugging:** Expect to encounter errors and issues while working on projects. Use these challenges as learning opportunities. Debugging and fixing errors will deepen your understanding of how AI models work.

- **Iterate and Improve:** Refine your models and approaches based on feedback and results. Iteration is a key part of the learning process.

Building a Curious Mindset

To cultivate a mindset that embraces and thrives on learning the basics, consider the following:

- **Stay Motivated:** Keep your curiosity alive by reminding yourself why you started learning AI. Set small milestones and celebrate your progress.

- **Connect with Others:** Join study groups or online communities where you can discuss AI concepts and share experiences.

- **Keep Exploring:** AI is a rapidly evolving field. Regularly explore new topics and advancements to stay engaged and motivated.

Summary

Chapter 2 has guided you through the fundamental concepts of AI, including machine learning, neural networks, and data science. By engaging with interactive learning tools, undertaking hands-on projects, and experimenting with different techniques, you lay a strong foundation for more advanced study.

Chapter 3: The Joy of Problem-Solving

Song: "Eye of the Tiger" by Survivor

AI is fundamentally about solving problems. Whether it's predicting outcomes, classifying data, or optimizing processes, the essence of AI lies in addressing and overcoming challenges. In this chapter, we'll explore how to approach problems methodically and embrace them as opportunities for growth and learning. The joy of problem-solving comes not just from finding solutions but from the entire journey of exploring, experimenting, and evolving.

The Essence of Problem-Solving in AI

1. **Understanding the Problem**

Before jumping into coding or model building, it's crucial to understand the problem you're trying to solve. A clear understanding of the problem helps in designing an effective solution. This involves:

- **Defining Objectives:** What are you trying to achieve? For instance, if you're working on a recommendation system, your objective might be to increase user engagement by suggesting relevant items.
- **Identifying Constraints:** What limitations do you have? These could be related to data quality, computational resources, or time constraints.

2. **Methodical Approach**

A methodical approach ensures that you address the problem systematically and effectively. Here's how to break down and tackle complex problems:

- **Problem Decomposition:** Break the problem into smaller, manageable parts. For example, if you're building a chatbot, decompose the problem into understanding user input, generating responses, and integrating with other systems.
- **Hypothesis Testing:** Formulate hypotheses about the problem and test them. For instance, if you're working on a classification problem, you might hypothesize that adding certain features will improve model performance.
- **Iterative Improvement:** Build and test prototypes or models iteratively. Start with a simple model, assess its performance, and refine it based on results.

3. **Problem-Solving Techniques**

Use various techniques and methodologies to approach and solve problems effectively:

- **Data Exploration:** Analyze and visualize the data to uncover insights and patterns. This helps in understanding the underlying structure and relationships in the data.
- **Feature Engineering:** Create new features from existing data to improve model performance. For example, you might create a feature representing the ratio of two existing features if it provides more meaningful information.
- **Algorithm Selection:** Choose appropriate algorithms based on the nature of the problem and data. Experiment with different algorithms to find the one that best addresses your problem.

Tips and Techniques for Effective Problem-Solving

1. Break Down Problems

Complex problems can be overwhelming, but breaking them down makes them more manageable:

- **Divide and Conquer:** Start by identifying the main components of the problem and address each component individually.

- **Set Milestones:** Define clear milestones and objectives for each part of the problem. This helps in tracking progress and maintaining focus.

- **Use Flowcharts:** Create flowcharts or diagrams to visualize the problem and solution process. This can help in organizing thoughts and identifying key steps.

2. Seek Feedback

Collaborating with others and seeking feedback can provide valuable insights and improve your solutions:

- **Peer Review:** Share your approach, code, or model with colleagues or peers. They can provide constructive feedback and suggest improvements.

- **Community Engagement:** Participate in forums, online communities, or study groups related to AI. Engaging with the community can expose you to different perspectives and solutions.

- **Mentorship:** Find a mentor who has experience in AI. They can guide you through complex problems and help you refine your approach.

3. Embrace Challenges

Challenges are opportunities for growth. Embrace them with a positive attitude:

- **View Challenges as Learning Opportunities:** Each challenge you encounter is a chance to learn something new. Approach problems with curiosity and a willingness to learn.

- **Stay Persistent:** Problem-solving can be frustrating at times. Stay persistent and keep experimenting until you find a solution.

- **Reflect on Successes and Failures:** After solving a problem, reflect on what worked well and what could be improved. This reflection helps in continuous learning and growth.

4. Use Problem-Solving Frameworks

Applying problem-solving frameworks can help structure your approach:

- **Root Cause Analysis:** Identify the underlying cause of the problem rather than just addressing symptoms. Tools like the "Five Whys" can help in root cause analysis.

- **Design Thinking:** Use design thinking to approach problems creatively. This involves empathizing with users, defining problems, ideating solutions, prototyping, and testing.

- **Agile Methodology:** Apply agile principles to work iteratively and adaptively. Agile practices like Scrum or Kanban can help in managing and solving complex problems.

Building a Joyful Mindset Towards Problem-Solving

To cultivate a mindset that finds joy in problem-solving:

- **Celebrate Small Wins:** Recognize and celebrate small successes along the way. This keeps you motivated and reinforces positive feelings towards problem-solving.

- **Stay Curious:** Maintain a curious and inquisitive mindset. Ask questions, explore different approaches, and remain open to new ideas.

- **Enjoy the Process:** Focus on the process of solving problems, not just the end result. Enjoy the journey of exploration, experimentation, and discovery.

Summary

Chapter 3 has highlighted the joy and satisfaction of solving problems in AI. By approaching problems methodically, breaking them down, seeking feedback, and embracing challenges, you can enhance your problem-solving skills and find joy in overcoming complex issues.

Chapter 4: The Power of Patterns

Song: "Shape of You" by Ed Sheeran

AI often revolves around the ability to recognize and interpret patterns within data. From detecting anomalies to predicting future trends, pattern recognition is at the core of many AI applications. This chapter delves into how identifying patterns can lead to significant breakthroughs and how understanding these patterns can enhance your AI projects.

The Significance of Pattern Recognition in AI

1. **Understanding Patterns**

At its heart, pattern recognition involves identifying regularities and structures within data. This can be anything from recognizing faces in images, understanding trends in time-series data, to detecting fraudulent transactions. Recognizing patterns allows AI systems to make sense of complex and often noisy data, leading to more accurate and actionable insights.

2. **Applications of Pattern Recognition**

- **Image and Speech Recognition:** AI systems can identify objects in images or understand spoken language by recognizing patterns in pixel values or audio signals.

- **Predictive Analytics:** By analyzing historical data, AI can recognize patterns that help predict future events, such as stock market trends or customer behavior.

- **Anomaly Detection:** Pattern recognition helps in identifying unusual data points or behaviors that deviate from established patterns, which is useful in fraud detection or quality control.

Tips and Techniques for Effective Pattern Recognition

1. Visualize Data

Data visualization is a powerful tool for identifying patterns and gaining insights into your data:

- **Use Visualization Tools:** Employ tools like Matplotlib, Seaborn, or Tableau to create visual representations of your data. Heatmaps, scatter plots, and histograms can reveal underlying patterns and correlations.

- **Explore Different Views:** Visualize data from multiple angles to uncover different types of patterns. For example, plotting time-series data can help identify trends and seasonality, while scatter plots can reveal relationships between variables.

- **Interactive Dashboards:** Create interactive dashboards that allow you to filter and manipulate data dynamically. This can help in discovering patterns that may not be apparent in static visualizations.

Example:

python

Copy code

```
import matplotlib.pyplot as plt
import seaborn as sns
import pandas as pd

# Sample data
```

```python
df = pd.read_csv('data.csv')

# Scatter plot
plt.figure(figsize=(10, 6))
sns.scatterplot(x='feature1', y='feature2', data=df, hue='target')
plt.title('Scatter Plot of Feature1 vs Feature2')
plt.show()

# Heatmap
plt.figure(figsize=(10, 8))
correlation_matrix = df.corr()
sns.heatmap(correlation_matrix, annot=True, cmap='coolwarm')
plt.title('Correlation Heatmap')
plt.show()
```

2. Experiment with Algorithms

Different algorithms are designed to handle patterns in data in various ways. Experimenting with different algorithms can help you understand how they recognize and leverage patterns:

- **Start with Simple Algorithms:** Begin with simpler models like linear regression or decision trees to understand how they handle patterns. These models provide a good baseline.

- **Try Complex Models:** Experiment with more advanced algorithms such as neural networks, clustering algorithms, or ensemble methods to see how they manage complex patterns. For instance, convolutional neural networks (CNNs) are particularly effective for pattern recognition in images.

- **Tune Hyperparameters:** Adjust hyperparameters to optimize how algorithms learn from patterns. Techniques like grid search or random search can help in finding the best parameters for your models.

Example:

python code

```python
from sklearn.model_selection import train_test_split, GridSearchCV
from sklearn.ensemble import RandomForestClassifier
from sklearn.neural_network import MLPClassifier

# Load data
X = df[['feature1', 'feature2', 'feature3']]
y = df['target']
X_train, X_test, y_train, y_test = train_test_split(X, y, test_size=0.2, random_state=42)

# Random Forest
rf = RandomForestClassifier()
rf.fit(X_train, y_train)
print('Random Forest Accuracy:', rf.score(X_test, y_test))

# Neural Network
nn = MLPClassifier()
nn.fit(X_train, y_train)
print('Neural Network Accuracy:', nn.score(X_test, y_test))

# Hyperparameter Tuning
param_grid = {'n_estimators': [50, 100, 200], 'max_depth': [None, 10, 20]}
grid_search = GridSearchCV(estimator=rf, param_grid=param_grid, cv=5)
grid_search.fit(X_train, y_train)
print('Best Parameters:', grid_search.best_params_)
```

3. Feature Engineering

Effective pattern recognition often relies on the quality of the features used. Feature engineering involves creating new features or modifying existing ones to better capture patterns:

- **Create Interaction Features:** Combine existing features to create new ones that may capture complex relationships. For instance, multiplying or adding two features might reveal new patterns.

- **Extract Temporal Features:** For time-series data, extract features like moving averages, trends, and seasonality to enhance pattern recognition.

- **Normalize and Scale:** Ensure that features are on a similar scale to help algorithms learn patterns more effectively.

Example:

python code

Creating interaction features

df['feature1_feature2'] = df['feature1'] * df['feature2']

Normalization

from sklearn.preprocessing import StandardScaler

scaler = StandardScaler()

df_scaled = scaler.fit_transform(df[['feature1', 'feature2', 'feature3']])

Building a Pattern Recognition Mindset

To harness the power of pattern recognition in AI:

- **Stay Observant:** Develop an eye for spotting patterns and anomalies in data. Cultivate a habit of questioning and exploring data deeply.

- **Be Patient:** Pattern recognition often involves trial and error. Be patient with the process and open to refining your approach.

- **Keep Learning:** Stay updated with advancements in algorithms and techniques for pattern recognition. Continuous learning helps in applying the latest methods to your problems.

Summary

Chapter 4 has highlighted the importance of recognizing and understanding patterns in data for AI. By visualizing data, experimenting with different algorithms, and engaging in effective feature engineering, you can enhance your ability to identify valuable patterns and improve your AI models.

In the next chapter, **Chapter 5: "The Art of Experimentation"**, we will explore the role of experimentation in AI development and how to effectively test and iterate on your models. Stay tuned and keep exploring the world of patterns!

Chapter 5: The Importance of Data

Song: "Counting Stars" by OneRepublic

Data is the foundation upon which AI models are built. From training machine learning algorithms to generating insights, data plays a crucial role in the success of any AI project. This chapter focuses on understanding different types of data, effective methods for data collection, and best practices for data cleaning and analysis.

Understanding Data Sources

1. **Types of Data**

AI relies on various types of data depending on the application:

- **Structured Data:** This is data that is organized into tables or spreadsheets, such as databases or CSV files. It includes data types like numbers, dates, and categorical labels.

- **Unstructured Data:** This data does not have a predefined format. Examples include text documents, images, audio files, and videos. It often requires more complex processing techniques to extract useful information.
- **Semi-Structured Data:** This data has some organizational properties but does not fit neatly into tables. Examples include JSON, XML, and log files.

Example:

- Structured Data: Sales records in a spreadsheet.
- Unstructured Data: Customer reviews from social media.
- Semi-Structured Data: Log files from web servers.

2. **Data Sources**
   - **Public Datasets:** Many organizations provide public datasets that can be used for training AI models. Examples include Kaggle, UCI Machine Learning Repository, and government databases.
   - **Web Scraping:** Collect data from websites using web scraping tools and libraries. Be mindful of the legal and ethical implications of scraping.
   - **APIs:** Use APIs provided by services like Twitter, Google Maps, or financial data providers to collect real-time or historical data.
   - **Surveys and Experiments:** Design and conduct surveys or experiments to gather specific data tailored to your project needs.

Example:

Python code

```
import requests

# Example API request
response = requests.get('https://api.example.com/data')
data = response.json()
```

Data Cleaning

1. **Importance of Data Cleaning**

Data cleaning is crucial because real-world data is often messy and incomplete. Cleaning data ensures that your AI models receive accurate and relevant information, which can significantly impact their performance.

2. **Common Data Cleaning Tasks**

    - **Handling Missing Values:** Fill in missing values with mean, median, or mode, or use imputation techniques. Alternatively, remove rows or columns with missing data if they are not critical.

    - **Removing Duplicates:** Identify and remove duplicate entries to avoid skewed analysis or redundant information.

    - **Correcting Errors:** Identify and correct inaccuracies or inconsistencies in the data, such as typos, incorrect values, or misformatted entries.

    - **Normalization and Scaling:** Ensure that numerical features are on a similar scale to improve model training and performance.

Example:

Python code

```python
import pandas as pd

from sklearn.impute import SimpleImputer

from sklearn.preprocessing import StandardScaler


# Load data
df = pd.read_csv('data.csv')


# Handle missing values
imputer = SimpleImputer(strategy='mean')
df['feature1'] = imputer.fit_transform(df[['feature1']])


# Remove duplicates
df = df.drop_duplicates()
```

```
# Normalize and scale
scaler = StandardScaler()
df[['feature1', 'feature2']] = scaler.fit_transform(df[['feature1', 'feature2']])
```

3. **Data Transformation**
    - **Feature Engineering:** Create new features that can improve model performance, such as aggregating data or encoding categorical variables.
    - **Data Aggregation:** Summarize data by grouping or aggregating to get a higher-level view of trends and patterns.
    - **Data Reduction:** Reduce the dimensionality of data using techniques like Principal Component Analysis (PCA) to focus on the most significant features.

Example:

Python code

```
from sklearn.decomposition import PCA

# Apply PCA
pca = PCA(n_components=2)
X_reduced = pca.fit_transform(df[['feature1', 'feature2', 'feature3']])
```

Analyzing Data

1. **Exploratory Data Analysis (EDA)**

EDA involves exploring and visualizing data to understand its structure, trends, and relationships:

- **Descriptive Statistics:** Use summary statistics to understand the central tendency, dispersion, and distribution of data.
- **Visualizations:** Create charts and plots to visually inspect the data and identify patterns or outliers.

Example:

Python code

```python
import matplotlib.pyplot as plt
import seaborn as sns

# Descriptive statistics
print(df.describe())

# Visualization
sns.pairplot(df[['feature1', 'feature2', 'target']], hue='target')
plt.show()
```

2. **Statistical Analysis**

Perform statistical tests to determine relationships between variables and validate hypotheses. Techniques include correlation analysis, hypothesis testing, and regression analysis.

Example:

Python code

```python
import scipy.stats as stats

# Correlation analysis
correlation_matrix = df.corr()
print(correlation_matrix)

# Hypothesis testing
t_stat, p_value = stats.ttest_ind(df['feature1'], df['feature2'])
print(f"T-statistic: {t_stat}, P-value: {p_value}")
```

Building a Data-Centric Mindset

To leverage the power of data effectively:

- **Be Thorough:** Pay attention to detail during data collection and cleaning. High-quality data leads to better AI models.

- **Stay Curious:** Continuously explore new data sources and techniques. Innovation often comes from experimenting with different data.

- **Collaborate:** Work with domain experts and data scientists to understand the context and improve data quality.

Summary

Chapter 5 emphasizes the critical role of data in AI. By understanding different data sources, mastering data cleaning techniques, and conducting thorough analysis, you can ensure that your AI models are built on a solid foundation of accurate and relevant data.

Chapter 6: Experimentation and Innovation

Song: "Rocket Man" by Elton John

Innovation in AI is driven by experimentation. The field is ever-evolving, and breakthroughs often come from trying new approaches and iterating on existing methods. This chapter focuses on the importance of experimentation in AI, encouraging you to explore different models, techniques, and innovations to find the best solutions for your projects.

---

1. Try Different Models

1. **Model Variety**

Different AI models have unique strengths and weaknesses, and the best choice depends on the specific problem you're addressing. Experimenting with various models can help you find the most effective approach.

- **Supervised Learning Models:** These models are trained on labeled data and include algorithms such as:

- **Linear Regression:** Used for predicting continuous values.
- **Logistic Regression:** Suitable for binary classification tasks.
- **Decision Trees and Random Forests:** Effective for both classification and regression.
- **Support Vector Machines (SVM):** Good for high-dimensional data and classification.
- **Gradient Boosting Machines (GBM):** Ensemble methods that build models sequentially to correct errors.

o **Unsupervised Learning Models:** These models find patterns in unlabeled data:
- **K-Means Clustering:** Groups data into clusters based on similarity.
- **Principal Component Analysis (PCA):** Reduces data dimensionality while retaining variance.
- **Hierarchical Clustering:** Builds a hierarchy of clusters.

o **Deep Learning Models:** These models are designed for complex tasks and large datasets:
- **Neural Networks:** Basic models that can be deepened for more complex problems.
- **Convolutional Neural Networks (CNNs):** Ideal for image and video processing.
- **Recurrent Neural Networks (RNNs):** Useful for sequential data like time series or text.

Example:

Python code

```
from sklearn.ensemble import RandomForestClassifier
from sklearn.svm import SVC
from sklearn.linear_model import LogisticRegression


# Define models
models = {
```

```python
    'Random Forest': RandomForestClassifier(),
    'SVM': SVC(probability=True),
    'Logistic Regression': LogisticRegression()
}

# Train and evaluate models
for name, model in models.items():
    model.fit(X_train, y_train)
    y_pred = model.predict(X_test)
    accuracy = accuracy_score(y_test, y_pred)
    print(f"{name} Accuracy: {accuracy}")
```

2. **Hyperparameter Tuning**

Adjusting the parameters of your models can significantly impact their performance. Techniques for hyperparameter tuning include:

- **Grid Search:** Systematically searches through a predefined set of hyperparameters.
- **Random Search:** Randomly samples from the parameter space to find optimal values.
- **Bayesian Optimization:** Uses probabilistic models to guide the search for optimal parameters.

Example:

Python code

```python
from sklearn.model_selection import GridSearchCV

# Define model and parameters
model = RandomForestClassifier()
param_grid = {'n_estimators': [10, 50, 100], 'max_depth': [None, 10, 20]}

# Grid Search
```

grid_search = GridSearchCV(model, param_grid, cv=5)

grid_search.fit(X_train, y_train)

Best parameters

print("Best parameters:", grid_search.best_params_)

---

2. Stay Updated

1. **Follow AI Research**

The field of AI is rapidly advancing, with new techniques and findings emerging regularly. Staying informed helps you incorporate the latest innovations into your work.

- **Read Research Papers:** Access platforms like Google Scholar, arXiv, and conference proceedings (e.g., NeurIPS, ICML).
- **Subscribe to AI Journals:** Follow leading AI journals and magazines for updates on breakthroughs and trends.

Example:

- Read papers on arXiv: arXiv AI Papers
- Explore AI news: AI News Sites

2. **Engage with the Community**

Participate in AI communities and forums to exchange ideas and stay up-to-date:

- **Online Communities:** Join platforms like Reddit's r/MachineLearning, Stack Overflow, and AI-specific forums.
- **Meetups and Conferences:** Attend local meetups, webinars, and international conferences to network and learn from experts.

Example:

- Attend conferences like CES or The AI Summit.
- Join online forums and discussion groups on platforms like LinkedIn or Twitter.

3. **Continuous Learning**

AI is a dynamic field, so ongoing education is vital:

- **Online Courses:** Take advanced courses on platforms like Coursera, edX, and Udacity.
- **Workshops and Bootcamps:** Participate in hands-on workshops and bootcamps for practical experience.

Example:

- Enroll in specialized courses on Coursera: AI and Machine Learning Courses

---

Building an Experimental Mindset

1. **Adopt a Growth Mindset**

Approach each experiment with the belief that learning and improvement are ongoing processes. Embrace failures as opportunities to learn and iterate.

- **Learn from Mistakes:** Analyze what went wrong and how to address it in future experiments.
- **Stay Curious:** Maintain a sense of wonder and curiosity about new methods and ideas.

2. **Document and Reflect**

Keep a detailed log of your experiments, including the models used, parameters tested, and results obtained. Reflect on what worked and what didn't to refine your approach.

Example:

- Use tools like Jupyter notebooks or a research journal to document your experiments and insights.

Summary

Chapter 6 highlights the importance of experimentation and innovation in AI. By trying different models, tuning hyperparameters, staying updated with the latest research, and engaging with the AI community, you can drive progress and discover effective solutions for your projects. Embrace the journey of experimentation as a path to growth and innovation.

Chapter 7: Collaboration

and Community

Song: "Lean on Me" by Bill Withers

AI is not a solitary journey; it thrives on collaboration and community engagement. Working with others can provide fresh perspectives, accelerate learning, and open up new opportunities for innovation. This chapter explores how joining communities, attending events, and collaborating with peers can enhance your AI journey.

---

1. Join Online Communities

1. Find Relevant Forums and Groups

Online communities are a great place to ask questions, share knowledge, and stay updated with the latest developments in AI. They offer a wealth of resources and diverse viewpoints that can enhance your understanding.

- **Reddit Communities:** Subreddits like r/MachineLearning, r/DataScience, and r/ArtificialIntelligence provide discussions on various AI topics and problems.
- **Stack Overflow:** Participate in the Machine Learning and Data Science tags to ask questions and provide answers.
- **LinkedIn Groups:** Join groups such as "Data Science & Machine Learning" or "Artificial Intelligence and Machine Learning" for professional discussions and networking.

Example:

Python code

```
# Example of a discussion post on Reddit
import requests
url = 'https://www.reddit.com/r/MachineLearning/.json'
response = requests.get(url, headers={'User-Agent': 'Mozilla/5.0'})
posts = response.json()['data']['children']
for post in posts:
    print(post['data']['title'])
```

2. **Engage in Discussions**

Actively participate in discussions to contribute your knowledge and learn from others. Share your projects, seek feedback, and help others with their questions. Constructive engagement can lead to meaningful collaborations and opportunities.

Example:

- Share your project on Reddit or Stack Overflow and ask for feedback.
- Offer to review or provide advice on others' projects.

2. Attend Meetups and Conferences

1. **Local Meetups**

Meetups offer a chance to connect with local AI enthusiasts, practitioners, and experts. They often include talks, workshops, and networking opportunities.

- **Meetup.com:** Find local AI and data science meetups to attend events and network with like-minded individuals.
- **University Events:** Many universities host AI talks, workshops, and seminars open to the public.

Example:

- Join a local AI or data science meetup group and attend regular events to stay connected with your community.

2. **National and International Conferences**

Conferences are excellent opportunities to learn about the latest research, trends, and technologies in AI. They also provide networking opportunities with experts and industry leaders.

- **Major Conferences:** Attend conferences like NeurIPS (Conference on Neural Information Processing Systems), ICML (International Conference on Machine Learning), and CVPR (Computer Vision and Pattern Recognition).
- **Workshops and Tutorials:** Participate in workshops and tutorials to gain hands-on experience and deeper insights into specific areas of AI.

Example:

- Register for a conference like NeurIPS and attend sessions on topics of interest. Network with speakers and attendees to exchange ideas and opportunities.

Building Collaborative Skills

1. Effective Communication

Good communication is key to successful collaboration. Be clear and concise when presenting your ideas and open to feedback.

- **Active Listening:** Pay attention to others' ideas and feedback to build a mutual understanding.
- **Clear Presentation:** Practice presenting your work in a way that is understandable to both technical and non-technical audiences.

Example:

- Create presentations or write articles about your projects to share with your community.

2. Collaborative Tools

Use collaborative tools to work efficiently with others on AI projects.

- **Version Control:** Tools like Git and GitHub help manage code changes and collaborate on projects.
- **Project Management:** Use platforms like Trello or Asana to track tasks and milestones in collaborative projects.

Example:
- Use GitHub to collaborate on open-source AI projects, review pull requests, and contribute to code repositories.

Embracing a Collaborative Mindset

1. **Be Open to Feedback**

Embrace feedback as an opportunity for growth. Be receptive to constructive criticism and use it to improve your work.

- **Seek Diverse Opinions:** Consult with peers from different backgrounds to gain diverse perspectives on your projects.
- **Iterate Based on Feedback:** Refine your work based on the feedback you receive to enhance its quality.

2. **Build and Maintain Relationships**

Networking is not just about exchanging business cards; it's about building and maintaining genuine relationships with others in the field.

- **Follow Up:** After meeting someone, follow up with a message or email to continue the conversation.
- **Offer Help:** Be willing to assist others with their projects and questions. Building a reputation as a helpful and knowledgeable person can lead to valuable connections.

Example:
- Attend a conference, meet several experts, and follow up with them via email or LinkedIn to discuss potential collaborations or opportunities.

Summary

Chapter 7 emphasizes the importance of collaboration and community in AI. By joining online communities, attending meetups and conferences, and building strong collaborative skills, you can enhance your AI journey and contribute to the collective growth of the field. Embrace the spirit of collaboration to learn from others, share your insights, and drive innovation in AI

Chapter 8: The Role of Ethics

Song: "Imagine" by John Lennon

AI technology is a powerful tool with the potential to impact societies in profound ways. As we harness its capabilities, it's essential to address the ethical implications of AI to ensure that it benefits humanity and respects fundamental rights. This chapter explores the role of ethics in AI and provides guidance on developing responsible AI systems.

---

1. Study AI Ethics

1. Understand Ethical Guidelines and Frameworks

Ethical guidelines and frameworks help navigate the complex moral landscape of AI development. Familiarize yourself with established guidelines and principles that promote fairness, transparency, and accountability in AI systems.

- o **Key Principles:** Look into principles such as fairness, accountability, transparency, and privacy. These principles guide the ethical development and deployment of AI technologies.
- o **Ethical Frameworks:** Study frameworks like the AI Ethics Guidelines from the European Commission or the IEEE's Ethically Aligned Design guidelines.

Example:

Python code

Example of a guideline reference

ethical_guideline = {

  "Fairness": "Ensure that AI systems do not discriminate against any individual or group.",

  "Transparency": "Provide clear explanations of AI decision-making processes.",

  "Accountability": "Assign responsibility for the outcomes of AI systems."

}

for principle, description in ethical_guideline.items():

  print(f"{principle}: {description}")

2. **Participate in Ethical Discussions**

Engage in discussions about AI ethics to understand various perspectives and deepen your knowledge. Forums, webinars, and academic papers are valuable resources for exploring ethical dilemmas and solutions.

- o **Online Courses and Workshops:** Enroll in courses focused on AI ethics to gain structured insights and practical knowledge.
- o **Academic Papers:** Read research papers on ethical AI to understand current debates and solutions.

Example:

- o Attend a webinar on AI ethics hosted by an academic institution or industry leader and participate in the Q&A sessions.

2. Consider Impacts

1. **Evaluate Societal Implications**

Assess how AI solutions impact individuals and society at large. Consider both the positive and negative effects of AI technologies on various groups and communities.

- **Impact Assessment:** Conduct impact assessments to evaluate how AI systems affect different stakeholders, including marginalized or vulnerable groups.
- **Long-Term Effects:** Think about the long-term consequences of AI technologies, including potential changes in job markets, privacy concerns, and social dynamics.

Example:

python

Copy code

```
# Example of an impact assessment
impact_assessment = {
    "Privacy": "Ensure that AI systems protect users' personal information and data.",
    "Employment": "Assess how automation might affect job opportunities in different sectors.",
    "Bias": "Identify and mitigate any biases that AI systems might perpetuate."
}
for area, consideration in impact_assessment.items():
    print(f"{area}: {consideration}")
```

2. **Design for Inclusivity**

Strive to design AI systems that are inclusive and accessible to diverse populations. Ensure that AI technologies serve all users fairly and equitably.

- **Inclusive Design:** Incorporate diverse perspectives in the design process to address the needs of different user groups.
- **Accessibility:** Make AI tools and applications accessible to people with disabilities or those from underrepresented backgrounds.

Example:

- Implement features in AI applications that consider various languages, accessibility needs, and cultural contexts.

Ethical Case Studies

1. **Real-World Examples**

Study real-world case studies of AI ethics to understand how ethical principles are applied in practice and learn from both successes and failures.

- **Case Study 1:** The ethical implications of facial recognition technology and its impact on privacy.
- **Case Study 2:** Bias in AI algorithms used in hiring processes and strategies for mitigating it.

Example:

- Analyze the controversies surrounding facial recognition and its ethical considerations.

2. **Learn from Industry Leaders**

Follow thought leaders and organizations that focus on ethical AI to stay informed about emerging issues and best practices.

- **Thought Leaders:** Follow experts such as Timnit Gebru, Kate Crawford, and the team at the [Partnership on AI](#).
- **Industry Initiatives:** Engage with initiatives that promote ethical AI practices, such as [AI Now Institute](#) and [Data & Society](#).

Example:

- Subscribe to newsletters or blogs from organizations like [AI Now Institute](#) to receive updates on ethical AI research and practices.

Developing an Ethical Mindset

1. **Reflect on Personal Values**

Reflect on your personal values and how they align with the ethical development of AI. Understanding your principles can guide your decisions and actions in AI projects.

- **Personal Reflection:** Consider what values are important to you (e.g., fairness, transparency) and how they influence your approach to AI.
- **Ethical Dilemmas:** Reflect on potential ethical dilemmas you might encounter and how you would address them.

Example:

- Write a personal statement on your ethical stance in AI and how you plan to uphold these values in your work.

2. **Promote Ethical Culture**

Foster a culture of ethics within your organization or community. Encourage discussions about ethical issues and advocate for responsible AI practices.

- **Ethical Guidelines:** Develop and share ethical guidelines within your team or organization.
- **Training and Awareness:** Provide training on AI ethics to raise awareness and build an ethical mindset among colleagues.

Example:

- Organize a workshop on AI ethics for your team to discuss best practices and ethical considerations in your projects.

Summary

Chapter 8 emphasizes the critical importance of ethics in AI development. By studying ethical guidelines, considering the societal impacts of AI, and fostering an ethical mindset, you can contribute to creating responsible and beneficial AI technologies. Embrace the principles of fairness, transparency, and inclusivity to ensure that AI serves humanity in a positive and equitable manner.

In the next chapter, **Chapter 9: "The Future of AI"**, we will explore the emerging trends and potential future developments in AI. Stay tuned to understand how the field is evolving and what lies ahead for AI enthusiasts and practitioners.

Chapter 9: The Future of AI

Song: "Don't Stop Believin'" by Journey

As AI continues to evolve at a rapid pace, it's essential to stay curious and proactive about its future directions. This chapter delves into the emerging trends and potential future advancements in AI, offering guidance on how to stay engaged and adaptable in this ever-changing field.

---

1. Follow Innovations

1. **Stay Informed About Emerging Technologies**

Keep yourself updated with the latest advancements in AI technology by following reputable sources and industry leaders. Innovations in AI often lead to new possibilities and applications.

- **Read Research Papers:** Regularly read academic journals and research papers to understand cutting-edge AI research. Platforms like arXiv and Google Scholar are valuable resources.
- **Subscribe to Newsletters:** Sign up for newsletters from AI research institutions, tech companies, and AI communities. Examples include The AI Weekly and Synced.

Example:

```python
# Example of staying updated with AI research
import requests
response = requests.get('https://arxiv.org/api/query?search_query=all:AI&start=0&max_results=5')
print(response.json())
```

2. **Engage with AI Conferences and Seminars**

Attend AI conferences, webinars, and workshops to learn about the latest advancements and network with experts in the field.

- **Major Conferences:** Participate in major AI conferences like NeurIPS, ICML, and CVPR to gain insights into the latest research and trends.
- **Online Webinars:** Join webinars and virtual events hosted by AI research organizations and tech companies.

Example:

- Register for the annual NeurIPS Conference and follow live streams or recordings of keynote speeches and research presentations.

3. **Explore Emerging AI Applications**

Look into new and innovative applications of AI across different domains, from healthcare to autonomous vehicles. Understanding how AI is being applied in diverse fields can spark ideas for future projects.

- **Healthcare:** AI-powered diagnostic tools and personalized medicine.
- **Autonomous Vehicles:** Advancements in self-driving car technology.
- **Environmental Monitoring:** AI for climate change analysis and environmental conservation.

Example:

- Read about the latest developments in AI for healthcare to explore new applications.

2. Be Adaptive

1. **Embrace Lifelong Learning**

The field of AI is continuously evolving, and lifelong learning is crucial to stay relevant. Adopt a mindset of continuous improvement and openness to new knowledge.

- **Online Courses and Certifications:** Enroll in advanced AI courses and earn certifications from platforms like Coursera, edX, and Udacity.
- **Skill Development:** Regularly update your skills by learning new programming languages, tools, and techniques relevant to AI.

Example:

python

Copy code

```
# Example of setting up a learning schedule
import datetime
today = datetime.date.today()
next_course_date = today + datetime.timedelta(days=30)  # Set a date for starting the next course
print(f"Start the next AI course on: {next_course_date}")
```

2. **Be Open to Change**

AI technologies and methodologies can change rapidly. Stay flexible and open to adapting your approaches and tools as new advancements emerge.

- **Experiment with New Tools:** Try out new AI frameworks, libraries, and tools that gain popularity. For example, experiment with new versions of TensorFlow or PyTorch.
- **Revise Techniques:** Regularly review and revise your techniques and methodologies based on new findings and advancements.

Example:

- Experiment with the latest version of TensorFlow to explore new features and improvements.

3. **Collaborate on Future Projects**

Collaborate with others on forward-looking AI projects to gain insights into emerging trends and contribute to innovative solutions.

- **Join Research Groups:** Participate in research groups or teams working on future AI technologies.
- **Collaborate on Open Source Projects:** Contribute to open source AI projects that are exploring new frontiers.

Example:

- Contribute to an open source AI project on GitHub that focuses on emerging AI applications.

Staying Curious and Engaged

1. **Set Personal Goals**

Set goals for yourself regarding learning and contributing to the field of AI. This can include goals for mastering new technologies, contributing to research, or developing innovative applications.

- **Learning Goals:** Set milestones for completing advanced courses or certifications.
- **Project Goals:** Aim to develop or contribute to a project that addresses a novel AI challenge.

Example:

- Define a goal to complete an advanced course on AI Ethics within the next six months.

2. **Foster a Growth Mindset**

Cultivate a growth mindset that embraces challenges and views setbacks as opportunities for learning. This mindset will help you navigate the ever-evolving landscape of AI with resilience and enthusiasm.

- **Embrace Challenges:** View complex problems as opportunities to grow and learn.

- **Reflect and Adapt:** Regularly reflect on your experiences and adapt your strategies to align with new insights and developments.

Example:
- Keep a journal of your learning experiences and challenges encountered, and review it regularly to adapt your approach.

Summary

Chapter 9 emphasizes the importance of staying curious and adaptable as AI continues to evolve. By following innovations, engaging with emerging technologies, and maintaining a growth mindset, you can remain at the forefront of AI advancements. Embrace lifelong learning and be open to change to thrive in the dynamic field of AI.

Chapter 10: Cultivating a Lifelong Curiosity

Song: "Forever Young" by Bob Dylan

Curiosity is not a destination but a lifelong journey. As you continue to delve into the field of AI, maintaining curiosity and enthusiasm is crucial for personal and professional growth. This final chapter provides practical strategies to help you cultivate a mindset of continuous learning and adaptability.

1. Set Learning Goals

1. **Create Short-Term and Long-Term Goals**

Establishing both short-term and long-term learning goals helps keep your curiosity alive and directs your focus. Short-term goals could be learning a new AI concept or tool, while long-term goals might involve mastering a specific area of AI or completing a significant project.

- **Short-Term Goals:** Aim to complete a course, build a small project, or read a few chapters of a relevant book within a specific timeframe.
- **Long-Term Goals:** Set goals such as earning a certification, publishing research, or developing a groundbreaking AI application over several months or years.

Example:

Python code

```
# Setting a short-term learning goal
import datetime
short_term_goal = {
    "Goal": "Complete TensorFlow Basics course",
    "Deadline": datetime.date(2024, 9, 30)
}
print(f"Short-Term Goal: {short_term_goal['Goal']} by {short_term_goal['Deadline']}")
```

2. **Track and Celebrate Achievements**

Regularly track your progress and celebrate your achievements, no matter how small. This practice helps you stay motivated and acknowledges your hard work.

- **Progress Tracking:** Use tools like journals or digital apps to record milestones and achievements.
- **Celebrations:** Reward yourself upon reaching goals, whether it's through relaxation, treating yourself, or sharing your success with others.

Example:

- Maintain a progress journal to document completed courses, projects, and new skills acquired.

---

2. Reflect and Iterate

1. **Regular Reflection**

Regular reflection on your learning journey allows you to evaluate what has worked, what hasn't, and how you can improve. Reflection helps in understanding your strengths and areas for growth.

- o **Reflective Journals:** Keep a journal where you document what you've learned, challenges faced, and insights gained.
- o **Self-Assessment:** Periodically assess your skills and knowledge to identify areas where you need further development.

Example:

Python code

```python
# Example of a reflective practice
from datetime import date
reflection = {
    "Date": date.today(),
    "Lessons Learned": "Understanding neural network architectures better.",
    "Challenges Faced": "Difficulty in tuning hyperparameters.",
    "Action Plan": "Research best practices for hyperparameter tuning."
}
print(reflection)
```

2. **Iterate on Learning Strategies**

Based on your reflections, adjust your learning strategies to address any gaps or to explore new areas of interest. Iteration helps refine your approach and keeps your learning journey aligned with your goals.

- o **Adjust Goals:** Modify your learning goals based on your progress and new interests.
- o **Change Methods:** Experiment with different learning methods, such as switching between reading, hands-on practice, and discussions.

Example:

- o If a particular learning method isn't effective, try integrating more interactive tools or hands-on projects into your routine.

Formula for Developing a Curious Mindset

1. **Start Small**

Begin with basic concepts and gradually progress to more advanced topics. Starting small makes the learning process manageable and builds a solid foundation.

- **Basic Concepts:** Focus on understanding fundamental principles before diving into complex topics.
- **Progressive Learning:** Incrementally build on your knowledge as you become more comfortable with the basics.

Example:

- Start with a beginner's course on machine learning and then move on to specialized topics like deep learning or reinforcement learning.

2. **Stay Engaged**

Keep yourself updated with the latest trends and innovations in AI. Staying engaged helps you remain relevant and excited about the field.

- **Follow Trends:** Subscribe to AI news sites, follow influential researchers, and participate in relevant forums.
- **Continuous Learning:** Regularly engage with new materials and technologies to stay current.

Example:

- Use platforms like ArXiv or AI Weekly to keep up with recent publications and advancements.

3. **Embrace Challenges**

View obstacles and challenges as opportunities for learning and growth. Embracing challenges helps you develop problem-solving skills and resilience.

- **Challenge Acceptance:** Take on difficult projects or problems that push your boundaries.
- **Learn from Failure:** Analyze setbacks to understand what went wrong and how you can improve.

Example:
- o If a project fails, conduct a post-mortem analysis to learn from the experience and apply those lessons to future projects.

4. **Seek Inspiration**

Find mentors, join communities, and be inspired by others' work. Inspiration can spark new ideas and motivate you to pursue your goals.

- o **Find Mentors:** Seek out mentors who can provide guidance and support.
- o **Join Communities:** Engage with AI communities, attend meetups, and collaborate on projects.

Example:
- o Participate in AI meetups or join online forums where you can interact with experts and enthusiasts.

5. **Reflect Often**

Regularly assess your progress, experiences, and learning strategies. Reflection helps in recognizing achievements, identifying areas for improvement, and refining your approach.

- o **Regular Reviews:** Schedule regular reviews of your learning goals and strategies.
- o **Feedback Collection:** Seek feedback from peers, mentors, or through self-assessment.

Example:
- o Set aside time each month to review your progress, update goals, and adjust strategies based on feedback and new insights.

Mindset Development Tips

1. **Passion Over Perfection**

Focus on your passion for learning rather than striving for perfection. Embracing your enthusiasm and curiosity will drive you to continue exploring and improving.

- **Passion Projects:** Work on projects that genuinely interest you, even if they are not perfect.
- **Celebrate Passion:** Enjoy the learning process and celebrate the progress you make, regardless of how close you are to perfection.

Example:

- Choose a project that aligns with your interests, such as developing an AI application for a cause you care about.

2. **Curiosity as a Habit**

Make curiosity a daily habit by dedicating time to explore new ideas, technologies, and concepts. Regular exploration keeps your curiosity alive and fuels your learning journey.

- **Daily Exploration:** Allocate time each day or week to read articles, watch videos, or work on projects related to AI.
- **Active Learning:** Engage actively with new materials and seek out opportunities to apply what you learn.

Example:

- Schedule a weekly routine for exploring new AI techniques or tools, such as experimenting with a new library or reading a research paper.

3. **Resilience**

Develop resilience to overcome setbacks and continue your learning journey. Resilience helps you bounce back from failures and remain motivated.

- **Perseverance:** Keep pushing forward despite challenges and setbacks.
- **Support Network:** Build a support network of peers and mentors who can offer encouragement and advice.

Example:

- After encountering a setback, reach out to a mentor for advice and use the experience as a learning opportunity to improve your approach.

Summary

Chapter 10 emphasizes the importance of cultivating a lifelong curiosity and developing a growth mindset to continue thriving in the field of AI. By setting learning goals, reflecting on progress, and embracing challenges, you can maintain enthusiasm and stay engaged with the evolving world of AI. Implementing the strategies and mindset tips outlined in this chapter will help you navigate your AI journey with passion and resilience.

As you embark on your lifelong learning journey, remember that curiosity is the driving force behind discovery and innovation. Stay curious, stay motivated, and let your passion for learning guide you to new heights in AI and beyond.

Conclusion: Embracing the Journey of Lifelong Curiosity

As we conclude this journey through the realms of artificial intelligence (AI), it's clear that curiosity is the driving force behind discovery, innovation, and personal growth. The chapters we've explored—each paired with a song that echoes its essence—serve as a guide to cultivating a deep and enduring passion for learning.

The Essence of Curiosity

Curiosity starts with a simple question and evolves into a profound quest for knowledge. It fuels our understanding and drives us to unravel the complexities of AI, transforming daunting concepts into exciting challenges. By embracing curiosity, we transform our learning journey into a fulfilling adventure.

Building a Strong Foundation

The chapters on embracing the basics and understanding data lay the groundwork for your AI journey. Recognizing patterns and solving problems are fundamental skills that enable you to navigate and innovate within the AI landscape. Each step, from mastering the basics to experimenting with new models, contributes to a robust understanding of AI.

The Role of Community and Ethics

AI is not an isolated field but one that thrives on collaboration and ethical considerations. Engaging with communities, sharing knowledge, and considering the ethical implications of AI are essential for responsible innovation. As you grow, remember that your work impacts not only the technology but also society at large.

Looking Ahead and Staying Engaged

The future of AI is brimming with possibilities. Staying curious about emerging technologies, adapting to changes, and setting new learning goals ensures that your journey remains dynamic and exciting. By embracing challenges and seeking inspiration, you keep the flame of curiosity alive.

Cultivating Lifelong Curiosity

Curiosity is a lifelong companion. It requires effort and dedication to maintain, but the rewards are profound. Set learning goals, reflect on your progress, and approach each challenge with resilience and passion. Make curiosity a habit and continuously seek new sources of inspiration.

As you move forward, remember the formula for developing a curious mindset: Start small, stay engaged, embrace challenges, seek inspiration, and reflect often. This approach will guide you in navigating the ever-evolving world of AI and beyond.

Final Thoughts

Curiosity is not just a trait but a mindset—a way of life. By nurturing this mindset, you open doors to endless possibilities and innovations. Embrace your journey with the knowledge that each question you ask and each challenge you tackle brings you closer to becoming an adept AI enthusiast and lifelong learner.

So, let curiosity be your guide, and may your journey through the world of AI be as rewarding as it is exciting. Keep asking questions, stay passionate, and remember: the adventure of learning never truly ends.

This conclusion wraps up the exploration of curiosity in AI, reinforcing the importance of continuous learning and the joy of discovery.

Glossary:

"Cultivating a Lifelong Curiosity":

1. **Curiosity**: The desire to learn and explore new knowledge and ideas continuously.

2. **Learning Goals**: Specific objectives set to guide and measure progress in acquiring new skills or knowledge.

3. **Reflection**: The process of reviewing and assessing one's experiences and progress to improve learning strategies.

4. **Resilience**: The ability to recover from setbacks and maintain motivation and enthusiasm.

5. **Adaptability**: The capacity to adjust and thrive in changing environments and evolving fields.

6. **Passion**: A deep-seated interest and enthusiasm that drives persistent learning and exploration.

7. **Mindset**: The mental attitude that influences how you approach learning and challenges.

These keywords encapsulate the core concepts of maintaining curiosity and fostering a growth mindset in your lifelong learning journey.

key points summarizing the journey to mastering AI through curiosity:

1. **Ignite Curiosity**: Begin by asking fundamental questions and exploring AI as a fascinating puzzle.

2. **Build a Strong Foundation**: Master basic AI concepts and engage in hands-on projects to solidify your understanding.

3. **Solve Problems Joyfully**: Approach AI challenges with a problem-solving mindset, breaking them down and seeking feedback.

4. **Recognize Patterns**: Develop skills in pattern recognition by visualizing data and experimenting with various algorithms.

5. **Value Data**: Understand the critical role of data in AI, focusing on effective collection, cleaning, and analysis.

6. **Innovate Through Experimentation**: Experiment with different models and stay updated with the latest research to drive innovation.

7. **Foster Lifelong Curiosity**: Set learning goals, reflect on progress, and continuously seek inspiration to maintain a curious and adaptive mindset.

www.ingramcontent.com/pod-product-compliance
Lightning Source LLC
Chambersburg PA
CBHW082240220526
45479CB00005B/1294